What's it like to be a...

BUS DRIVER

Written by Judith Stamper
Illustrated by T.R. Garcia

Troll Associates

Special Consultant: Charles Flateman, *Vice President, Hudson Transit Lines, Inc.*

Library of Congress Cataloging-in-Publication Data

    What's it like to be a bus driver / by Judith Stamper;
illustrated by T.R. Garcia.
        p.   cm.—(Young careers)
    Summary: Describes the work done by a bus driver as he picks up
his bus, checks it out, and follows his morning route.
    ISBN 0-8167-1795-8 (lib. bdg.)   ISBN 0-8167-1796-6 (pbk.)
    1. Bus drivers—Juvenile literature. 2. Bus driving—Vocational
guidance—Juvenile literature. [1. Bus drivers. 2. Occupations.]
I. Garcia, T. R., ill. II. Title. III. Series.
HD8039.M8S73 1990
388.3´22044´02373—dc20   89-34388

What's it like to be a...

BUS DRIVER

Charlie Johnson is a city bus driver. His day begins at 7:00 A.M. at the big station on Main Street.

"Morning, Charlie," the dispatcher calls out. The dispatcher is in charge of sending out each bus on time.

"Morning," Charlie says with a smile. "Where's my bus?"

"Out in the yard," the dispatcher answers. "It just got a new front tire."

FIRST AID

"Thanks," Charlie says. He takes his day card from the dispatcher.

Charlie keeps a record of his route on the day card. He lists all the places where his bus will stop.

DAY CARD
CHARLIE

Out in the yard, Charlie finds his bus. He waves to the mechanics, who are busily fixing another bus.

Charlie checks his watch. The time is 7:10. His route begins at 7:30. Before then, he must check out his bus. Charlie opens the door and climbs inside. He slips behind the wheel. He switches on the buttons that start the bus's air pressure building.

A big bus uses air pressure to work its brakes and windshield wipers. The pressure also opens the bus door. It takes about twenty minutes for the air pressure to build up.

HAVE A NICE

Charlie looks at his day card. He will drive along route number 7 today. Charlie's bus has an electronic sign in front. He dials in the route number on a small computer.

The sign on the front of the bus flashes on: NO. 7. MAIN STREET STATION TO FAR HILLS. Then it flashes another message: HAVE A NICE DAY.

Charlie starts up the engine. He looks at the dials on the dashboard. The readings are all correct.

NO 7 MAIN STREET STATION TO FAR HILLS

Next, he makes sure all the lights are working.

It is 7:30. Charlie writes the time on his day card. Then he pulls out of the station.

Charlie's first stop is on Main Street. He arrives at exactly 7:35. Several people are waiting at the bus stop. Some are men and women on their way to work. Others are girls and boys on their way to school.

"Good morning," Charlie says to his first passenger. The passenger tells the driver where he wants to go. Charlie tells him what the fare is.

The bus driver's busy day has begun.

Charlie has many different jobs to do. He must answer the passengers' questions. A driver must know the names of every street along his route. He must be polite and helpful.

Exact-Fare Machine

TAKE TRANSFER

A

B

Transfers

Charlie also must know how much each ride costs. He takes the fare money from each passenger and gives out change. Some buses have exact-fare machines, and passengers cannot get change. When they get on the bus, they must know how much the ride costs, so they can put the right amount into the exact-fare machine.

At each stop, Charlie picks up passengers or drops them off. He pulls up at the curb and opens the door. He waits until everyone is in or out. Then he closes the door again.

Charlie's most important job is driving safely. He has to steer the big bus through heavy traffic.

A bus driver must know all about traffic signs and rules. He has to signal when he turns or stops.

Stopping a big bus takes skill. Charlie knows exactly when to put on the brakes to make the bus stop at the right time.

Charlie has been trained to drive in all kinds of weather. When it rains, he turns on the windshield wipers. He is extra careful when driving on wet streets.

Snowy weather means dangerous driving. Charlie knows how to brake on ice. He knows what to do if his bus gets stuck in the snow.

But Charlie doesn't have to worry about snow today! It's a clear, sunny morning, and Charlie has no trouble keeping his bus on schedule. He tries to arrive at each stop at a certain time. He cannot be too early or too late.

Charlie's bus moves along its route.
Passengers get on and get off.

"Quickly, now," Charlie says to one group of passengers. "We don't want to be late for school!"

The boys and girls hurry onto the bus. They ride Charlie's bus to school every day.

Charlie smiles at them.

"Wish me good luck," one boy says to Charlie. "I have a spelling test in school today!"

At another stop, an elderly man is waiting. He cannot climb up the high first step. Charlie's bus is a kneeling bus. Charlie lets out some air pressure. The bus "kneels" down for this special passenger.

By 9:00 A.M., Charlie reaches the end of his route. All the passengers get off the bus.

Charlie picks up his day card. He writes down the time. He lists how many people rode the bus and how much money he took in. He notes down any problems with the bus.

Charlie stands up to stretch. It's time for a short break.

Ten minutes later, Charlie reaches up to the sign computer. He punches in new numbers.

Outside on the bus, the sign flashes on: No. 7. FAR HILLS TO MAIN STREET STATION.

Charlie gets into the driver's seat again. He turns the bus around for its return trip.

Have a nice day, Charlie.